Sources of Power

Robert Boysen

Sources of Power

ISBN 978-1506-903-20-0 PRINT
ISBN 978-1506-903-21-7 EBOOK

LCCN 2016955758

October 2016

Published and Distributed by
First Edition Design Publishing, Inc.
P.O. Box 20217, Sarasota, FL 34276-3217
www.firsteditiondesignpublishing.com

Table of Contents

I can calculate the motion of heavenly bodies, but not the madness of people.

-- Isaac Newton

Birth of a Theory

Sometime during the middle of the 20th century, many engineering educators decided that engineering students were being instructed too narrowly. As a result of this decision, several American universities adopted five-year engineering curricula. The benefit of these curricula was that they offered the engineering student the possibility of earning two bachelor's degrees --- one in the arts (BA) and one in science (BS) --- with only five years of effort. However, these curricula never became very popular. The relatively free market in engineering job opportunities at the time persisted in valuing a master's degree much more than two undergraduate degrees. In addition, the typical five-year curriculum was more intensive than the typical four-year curriculum. Few students wanted to make the extra effort and take the extra time involved to complete the longer course of study.

Since I was an open-minded teenager, raised in a household of skeptics, I decided to take advantage of the education offered by a five-year engineering program. Thus began my exposure to a broad range of academic pursuits. The university I attended (Rutgers) had thousands of students. My class had 360 people who had chosen to major in engineering. However, only five out of these 360 engineering students were pursuing five-year degrees. There were no comparable programs anywhere in the university. In some ways, the five of us were like a missing link between disciplines.

Being exposed to a wide variety of courses at the same time resulted in some very odd juxtapositions. For example, one day, I attended a Psychology 101 lecture on how human ethics are developed and determined. I then crossed the campus and participated in a Philosophy recitation regarding various opinions on what human ethics "ought to be." Compared to the usual approach of science courses I was taking, however, this seemed very strange. When I learned about Newton's second law of motion, for instance, no one showed the slightest desire to discuss what it "ought to be."

In subsequent years, I learned that my psychology professor was a bit ahead of his time. The theories he used in his lecture to a group of sophomore undergraduates were both controversial and new, just in the process of being developed by J. Bowlby and others during the early second half of the 20th century. And, of course, when Newton first put forward his laws of motion, it is likely that there were quite a few philosophers who were willing to discuss what the second law of motion ought to be.

Although I did not realize it at the time, I was experiencing the gradual demise of philosophy as a highly practical and relevant discipline. When the ancient Greeks first labeled themselves as "Lovers of Knowledge" (*philo sophia*), they were referring to knowledge of all things. However, in a process that accelerated rapidly during and after the Renaissance, important portions of human knowledge became based on definitive confirmation by observation and experiment. As a result, the concept that some knowledge is no longer in the purview of philosophy became widely accepted. "Proven" knowledge moved into a separate category, one which we label "science" today.

As this process progressed, the scope of philosophy - in which reasoned opinions are valued as much as confirmed hypotheses - became narrower and narrower. Simultaneously, the scope of the sciences – with its experimentally proven facts - became broader and broader. This change in accepted thought processes is the hallmark of the Enlightenment – the grand flowering of the human intellect since the Renaissance. It may be philosophy's gradual diminution as the all-important mental discipline, but it is also its greatest success. It gave birth to all of science.

In this treatise, I am attempting to enhance this trend of moving accepted knowledge of human nature from the realm of philosophy to that of science. Creation of a general theory of human nature is the first step in this process. It will require a great deal of testing and development via thought experiments and hands-on experimentation. All of these later steps are beyond the scope of this treatise.

The thoughts that comprise this theory are based on the exceptionally broad exposure I have had to a wide variety of academic and cultural experiences. The development of this theory resulted from the combination of key concepts from evolution theory, Freudian psychology, cultural anthropology, and sociology. Additional academic sources of concepts included history, management theory, political science, and economics.

In addition to this broad academic background, I have been influenced by extensive people management experience in both my professional life and in non-profit management activities. I have also been exposed to a wide variety of cultures during my extensive travels (60 countries, including 30 countries by bicycle).

After combining the concepts relevant to human nature that I learned as a result of my broad experience and exposure to different cultures, I added several key observations of my own.

Finally, I developed the implications of this broad combination of concepts to derive a general theory of human nature.

The treatise contains no new knowledge, only a general theory. My work in formulating this theory is only a first step in the overall process. My hope is that others will be inspired to do the thought experiments and experimental investigation work required to confirm, deny, or modify the theory.

Life is really simple, but we insist on making it complicated.

-- Confucius

Hypothesis

The human race has turned the evolutionary process upside down. Originally, the environments in which humans lived naturally selected individuals to continue the species through procreation. However, that is no longer the case. At this point in time, human beings have significantly increased their capabilities so that they now control, influence, dictate, and select their own environments. As a result, they also decide which individuals will procreate the species, how many individuals will be born, and when and even how they will be created.

At this moment, my personal environment consists of my computer, desk, climate-controlled house, and culturally-appropriate clothing. When I decide to stop my writing for the day, my environment will expand to include a recliner chair, a television set, a dog, and a partner with whom to have a conversation. Earlier today, my environment consisted of a climate-controlled car, a flower garden, a doctor's office, a comfortable restaurant, and other conversational partners.

All of these environmental elements were created by human beings; they were not the result of the vagaries of the physical universe.

The element that had the greatest chance of terminating my existence was the time I spent driving my climate-controlled car. However, if that event had taken place, the trigger would almost certainly have been human error – either my own error or the error of another human being. Either through a conscious act or inadvertently, human beings routinely create the vast majority of their own environments.

Ironically, the process of evolution has created a creature – the human being – whose primary motivation is to escape the process that created it. To a very large extent, humans are now able to control their environment rather than needing to adapt to it. Only an environmental cataclysm of the greatest proportion has the potential to return the human race to the mode of being naturally selected by its environment. In the future, even that possibility is likely to be removed. The ability to control the results of even a cataclysmic event is conceivable now; in time, it will probably become a reality.

One other way that human beings currently control their environment is to physically move to more hospitable climates. For example, some people (known as "snowbirds") move south in the winter and north in the summer. In the foreseeable future, our ability to control our environment should expand even further; we should one day be able to choose the planet on which we wish to live.

Control of the environment is a key factor that separates human beings from other species. Of course, members of other species also attempt to control their environments. Every time a creature builds a nest, uses a tool, or migrates, it is trying to improve upon the environment in which it finds itself. However, the difference between those attempts and the actions of human beings can be measured by the level, the complexity, and the success of environmental control. The routine accomplishments of humans vis à vis their environment are so many orders of magnitude greater than other species as to be on a different plane. Natural selection would easily come into play for the simple nest builder with a small environmental change. On the other hand, as noted above, a major environmental cataclysm would be required for natural selection to again become an influential factor in human development.

Perhaps I am being a bit too optimistic about humankind. My model of human behavior, however, is not based on the least powerful of current human cultures. Rather, this model is based on the assumption that the most powerful current examples of human nature represent our future. Whether or not humankind succeeds in the long run, however, there remains little doubt that its current all-consuming focus is the control of various aspects of its environment.

The hypothesis presented in this work is as follows:

> *All of human nature is powered exclusively by two motivations:*
>
> *1) the motivation to procreate the species;*
>
> *2) the motivation to control its own environment in order to survive to procreate.*

To put it in more colloquial terms, people are motivated exclusively by sex and power.

All human activities are the result of these two motivating factors. Human beings select and control their environment in order to ensure survival.

The procreation process in human beings consists of two phases. The first phase involves the physical maturation of the individual to the point that he or she is able to conceive the next generation. The second phase requires the individual to survive long enough to nurture his or her resulting offspring to the same level. Human offspring must be nurtured in order to survive to maturity. In order to successfully complete both phases, the total survival time needed for the human procreation process is approximately thirty to forty years.

The long-term history of human progress is essentially a history of gaining greater power over and ever-increasing scope of control of the human environment. For example, shelter for humans began in caves. Over time, humans learned to construct structures out of mud and animal hides. In the modern era, those shelters provided increasing levels of protection through the use of stone, concrete, and the building materials we use today. Similarly, in ancient Rome, 80 to 90 percent of the population needed to be involved in supplying sufficient food for the populace. Today, only 2 to 3 percent of the labor force needs to be involved in production of the food supply in advanced economies.

Humans have also increased their comfort level over time through a variety of inventions. Even something as basic as furniture progressed from the use of hides on the ground to wood stools to cushioned chairs and beds. Our ability to communicate with one another progressed from the use of human messengers to clay tablets to the printing press. In the modern era, we have seen an explosion of electronic devices that allow us to maintain instant contact with people around the globe. We have also progressed from using our own feet as the primary mode of transportation to the use of beasts of burden to sailing ships to aircraft. Advances in medical technology have also dramatically increased the expected life spans of human beings over those of their predecessors. We could easily point to countless other examples of human progress over time. Each of these represents an advance in the ability of human beings to control their environments.

The major difference between human beings and most other forms of life as we know it is the relationship to the evolutionary process. Most forms of life survive by adapting to their environment one way or another. Human beings, on the other hand, have not evolved significantly for many thousands of years. Instead, every day humans learn more about how to control their environments and, therefore, how to exert power over them.*

At this point, most readers will find this hypothesis to be extremely cynical. However, this treatise fully recognizes and embraces the more positive aspects of humankind as well.

Of course, humans are also motivated by factors such as love or friendship, empathy, and religion and/or morality. In addition, they have altruistic feelings for fellow humans, even fellow species. Inspired leadership can motivate people; even art and other forms of expression can motivate.

Human beings acquire all of these motivators through membership in a society. As evidenced by the massive variation in cultural values and mores that exist between various human societies, all of them are aspects of human cultures, rather than in-born qualities. Additional proof is the fact that these motivators are all absent in one month olds. Altruistic very young infants do not exist. Acquiring the culture of a society is simply an extremely important and powerful way that human beings enhance their power over their environments.

**Basic human nature has remained the same over a long period of time. One can find evidence in the art, construction, and human relations of ancient Egyptians from 5,000 or more years ago (at least 250 generations). The basic nature of those Egyptians is virtually identical to human nature today.*

How do these "cultural motivators" become part of the human experience? The process of enculturation occurs chiefly in the subconscious and chiefly during an individual's childhood. In order to obtain membership in good standing in a human society and, therefore, gain the massive enhancement of power over the environment that results, an individual must undergo successful enculturation. In more colloquial terms, this process provides the individual with the necessary "ticket" to succeed. When this enculturation process fails, the result can be disastrous. In earlier times, people who did not successfully obtain these cultural motivators were thought to be possessed by the devil. In modern times, we refer to them as sociopaths or psychopaths.

The motivation that has made enculturation an almost universal human phenomenon is the drive to survive via the acquisition of power—the power that can only be achieved via membership in a society.

In summary, membership in a society vastly enhances the power of individuals to survive to successful procreation. To become a member of a particular society, the individual must be enculturated by it. Enculturation occurs early in life and is chiefly absorbed on a subconscious level.

Words are, of course, the most powerful drug used by mankind.

--Rudyard Kipling

Key Definitions

Several terms which appear frequently in this work are used in a much broader sense than is the colloquial norm. Following is an alphabetical listing of these terms and the definitions as used here:

Beliefs – Presumed knowledge that fills the gap between parts of the environment that an individual can control (via rational thought or physical/instinctive properties) and the individual's total environment. One example is religious beliefs. Belief is "knowledge" not supported by a preponderance of evidence.

Culture – A set of appropriate modes of action and beliefs that are implanted in the subconscious or conscious mind by the socialization process of the relevant society. The customs, arts, social institutions, behavior, ethics, religion, and attitudes of a social group.

Emotions – All non-rational aspects of the human mind. This broad definition includes such traditional emotions as fear, love, hate, disgust, and contentment. In addition, it includes physically-driven "feelings" such as hunger, thirst, and sex drive, as well as psychological needs such as self-worth, propriety, freedom, and power. Any non-rational ramification of the human mind is an emotion by this definition. Feelings are a subset of emotions.

Environment – Everything that is external to an individual that has either a potential or an actual effect on that individual. Includes the physical environment, the human environment, animal and plant environments, and any virtual environment (such as religious faith) that is based on belief systems. God is part of the true believer's environment.

Knowledge – The ability to predict the outcomes of actions and environmental events, either to a certainty or within a stated statistical probability. Knowledge can be either conscious or subconscious. It includes logic, technology, mathematics, physics, chemistry, history, psychology, probability and statistics, and other similar disciplines. The boundaries between knowledge and belief are a consistent and universal source of controversy. These boundaries have not been and probably never will be well defined. However, a consensus can be agreed upon in most cases.

Power – The ability to exert control, either partially or fully, over any aspect of an individual's environment. It includes the concept of mere influence.

Procreation – Sexual reproduction of the species. Procreation is motivated by both the desire to engage in sexual relations and an inherent desire to produce offspring and thereby ensure the continuation of the species.

Reproduction – Development of a viable next generation of a species. It consists of two universal elements: conception leading to birth, and the process of nurturing and raising the offspring. The desire to engage in sexual relations is a human driver; the process of nurturing and raising offspring is a human instinct.

Socialization/Enculturation – The process of implanting a culture's norms into an individual's mind, either subconsciously or consciously. This process normally takes place during early life. Failure of this process can lead to serious psychological deficits, often resulting in socio-pathology and/or psychopathology. Socialization/enculturation is often referred to as the development of a conscience.

Society -- Any group of human beings who have a significant effect upon an individual, especially during his or her formative years. The size, definition, and locale of the group can range from all of humankind to one's immediate family, depending on the context. Communication among members of a society can include forms other than direct human contact, such as printed and electronic media in word and image.

Species – A group of living individuals who are or have been capable of reproduction with each other under appropriate conditions. This definition results in far fewer species than the one in popular use. For example, pet dogs, wild dogs, foxes, wolves, and coyotes are all considered to be members of the same species.

Everything in the world is about sex except sex, Sex is about power.

-- Oscar Wilde

Explanations & Observations

A Snapshot of Human Nature

Any attempt to understand human nature in the broadest sense must include the following two significant concepts:

1) There are only two basic human drives: the drive to reproduce (the sex drive) and the drive to control the individual's environment to the point at which successful reproduction can take place. (See "Basic Drives" below.)

2) Emotions are the sole ultimate driving force for human actions; rational thought processes are merely the tools that human beings use in order to satisfy a spectrum of immediate and probable future emotions. (See "Emotions Motivate Action" below.)

A great deal of study and research has focused on topics that are all part of human nature. These topics include human cultures, sex drives, physical attributes, instincts, socialization, and the definition of knowledge. In addition, researchers in a variety of academic disciplines, such as sociology, psychology, neurology, anthropology, medicine, philosophy, and biology, have investigated these topics in recent decades.

This work represents an attempt to create a general and broad understanding of human nature by combining the two concepts outlined above with these current popular topics related to human nature. As one might expect, the result is a fairly complex hypothesis. The following flow chart, which presents the hypothesis as a "snapshot" of human nature, was developed to help simplify and aid in the understanding of this material. The discussions that follow look at each of the elements and relationships shown on the flow chart.

A good sketch is better than a long speech

--Napoleon Bonaparte

A Flow Chart of Human Nature

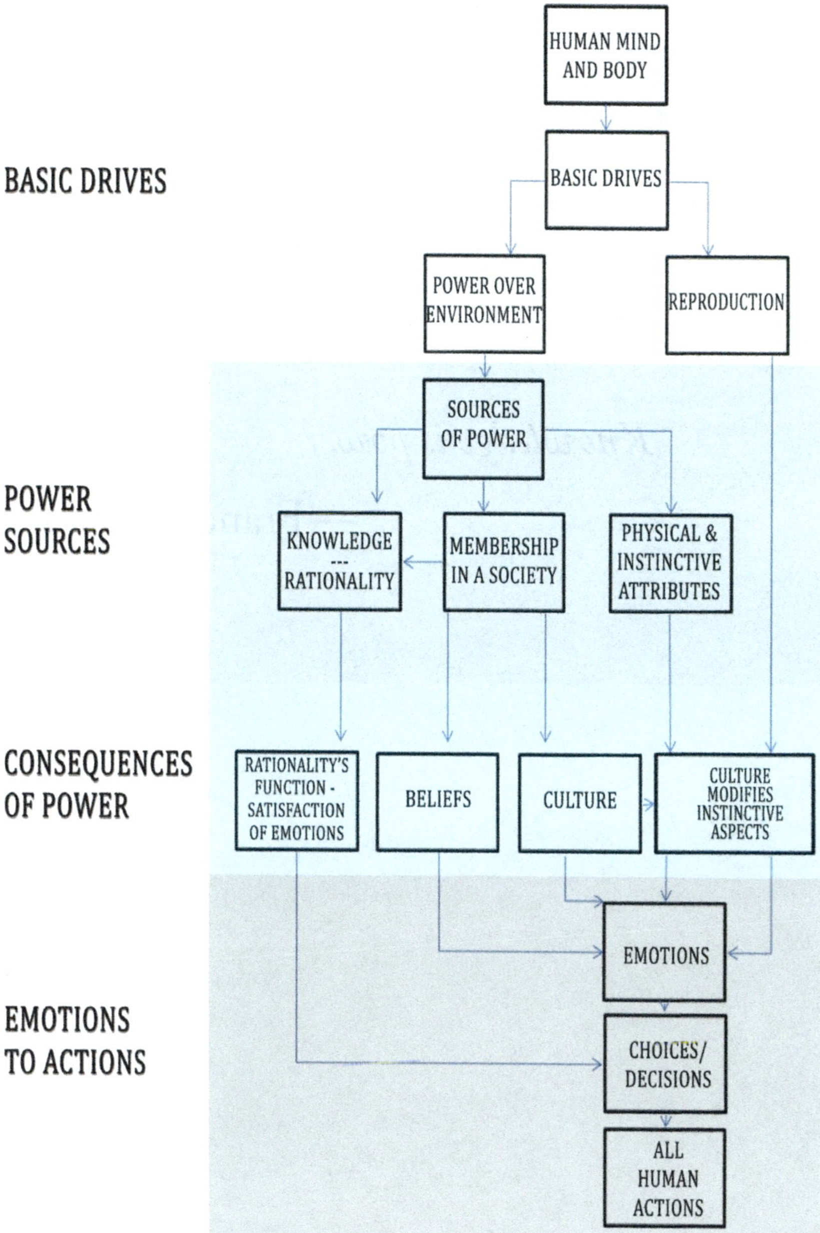

Knowledge is power

-- Francis Bacon

Basic Drives

The following sections of text refer to the corresponding boxes on the flow chart on the preceding page.

Reproduction

If the basic drives of any organism are not fully focused on survival of the species, then that species will surely not survive in the long term. Since all organic life as we know it ages and eventually dies, it is imperative for a species' survival that it has a basic drive to reproduce new individuals which in turn have the capability of reproduction. So it is for the human species. A great deal of research, theory, and discussion has been dedicated to the human drive to reproduce. It does not need elaboration here.

Power Over the Environment

The drive to reproduce, however, requires that the individual survive long enough to accomplish the act. The second basic human drive, therefore, is to control the environment in such a way as to allow for survival to successfully reproduce. Reproducing new members of the species that are in turn capable of reproduction will not ensure the survival of the species unless those new members also survive long enough to reproduce successfully. So another piece of this drive is ensuring survival into the third generation.

The time of survival required for continuing successful reproduction in humans is quite long, particularly when the time required to successfully nurture offspring is included. An initial period of 15 to 20 years is required for an individual to reach the age of reproductive capability. A second period of 15 to 20 years is needed in order to nurture the offspring to the age of reproductive capability. As a result, the total reproductive cycle requires a period of 30 to 40 years.

Different species reach the goal of surviving long enough to reproduce successfully in a variety of ways. Some of the methods of ensuring successful reproduction include: flexibility/adaptation to changes in the environment, rapid reproduction that may include multiple births, a lack of a nurturing period for offspring, and rapid evolution.

The human species has taken a different path, however. Unlike any other species, humans have been able to survive over a very long time period due to the ability of individual members of the species to CONTROL their environment. As noted above, this need to control the individual's environment is the second basic drive of all human beings. Both individuals and human societies play a major role in determining the survival of individual members and human beings as a whole. Unique to the human species is the fact that the environment is no longer in control; human beings are in control.

Reason is an excellent thing, ...but reason... satisfies only the rational side of man's nature. While will is a manifestation of...the whole human life including reason and all the impulses.

--Fyodor Dostoyevski

Sources of Power

In order to gain control over anything, one needs to be able to exercise power over it. The basic sources of human power can be categorized into the following three parts:

1) Physical and Instinctive aspects

Physical and instinctive aspects of a human being are obvious sources of an individual's power over his or her environment. Some examples of physical aspects include the instinct to defend oneself, to attack when necessary, to gather food, and to obtain shelter. Many other examples exist. These instinctive reactions to common needs, dangers and frustrations do not involve cognitive functions and are common to all higher forms of animal life. They are powerful mechanisms for individual survival.

Through his or her physical abilities, an individual can create objects and perform actions to satisfy a wide range of emotions/feelings.

2) Knowledge and Rationality

The second major source of human power is knowledge and rationality, the ability to predict the outcome of actions and environmental events. It is related to membership in a society - the third source of power - in that society membership facilitates the transmission of knowledge from individual to individual, from society to society, and from generation to generation.

The ability to predict outcomes of actions and events allows human beings to gain control of those outcomes.

3) Membership in a Society

Membership in a society causes personal power to be enhanced tremendously. Power is enhanced directly via joint action that society membership promotes. Protection and predictive capabilities are vastly enhanced as well. Finally, as discussed elsewhere in this treatise, the phenomenon of gaining ever-increasing knowledge as it is passed down from generation to generation is unique to human cultures and is an immense source of power.

Understanding the culture of a society also vastly enhances an individual's ability to predict the actions of his or her fellow society members. As noted above, the ability to predict outcomes allows for control of those outcomes.

Every addition to true knowledge
is an addition to human power
-- Horace Mann

Consequences of the Sources of Power

The Function of Knowledge/Rationality

Through the rational thinking process, knowledge allows an individual to predict the results of his or her own actual, current, future, or hypothetical actions, as well as the actions of other people. It also allows an individual to predict consequences of changes in his or her environment. The rules of rational thought are unchanging. They are hard wired in all human beings of "normal" mental capacity, but they are often overwhelmed by the influence of strong emotions.

All predictions have a probability of being correct or incorrect. For example, there is a high probability that a prediction that the sun will rise tomorrow will be correct. However, a prediction that a newborn in the United States will live 78 years only has a probability of approximately 50 percent. And, a prediction that rainfall in New York City in July 2017 will exceed 10 inches has a very low probability of being correct.

The rational thought process can also predict an individual's future emotions. To a large extent, the ability to predict them allows for optimizing the satisfaction of both current and future emotions. For human beings, rational thinking is the "tool" used to make action choices that lead to this outcome. The ability to use the rational thought process in this way seems to be a power that is largely limited to the human species.

All action decisions are based on spectrums of current and probable future emotions. All decisions are "emotional"; there are no "rational" decisions. When a decision is colloquially labeled as "emotional," it actually means that the decision does not take sufficient account of potential future emotions as opposed to immediate emotions. On the other hand, when a decision is colloquially labeled "rational," it means that a good balance between probable future and current emotions has been achieved in making that decision.

However, the emotions that motivate any decision are usually a complex combination of current and probable future emotions with varying degrees of need and priority — i.e., a spectrum of both types of emotions. Individuals use the rational thought process to sort out these often competing emotional needs so that they can optimize their actions.

Unfortunately, the process is not perfect and it usually occurs subconsciously. A key factor in the process is the relative weight that an individual gives to current versus probable future emotions. If he or she only gives weight to current emotions in the decision-making process, then that individual is essentially behaving in the same way as any of the higher animals.

For example, a dog acts almost purely on current emotions with no valuation given to probable future emotions. If he yields to the current emotion of wanting to eat the steak he sees on his owner's table, he does so because he has no understanding that his future emotions may suffer greatly as a result of this behavior; his owner is likely to keep him caged in the future when he is alone in the house to prevent a recurrence of this act.

The ability to predict and consider probable future emotions in making action decisions is the essence of being human.

Culture and Enculturation

An individual's membership in society greatly enhances his or her power to control his or her environment. A human who is totally removed from society would be in great danger of not being able to reproduce the species. That individual would find it almost impossible to survive and reproduce without the knowledge, lessons, and cooperative interactions which society provides.

However, members in a society must adhere to certain behavior restrictions, rules, norms, and regulations in order for the society itself to be successful. Just as individual species evolve, so too do societies and cultures, and the fittest cultures are the ones that survive.

Social animals, including human beings, have evolved mechanisms of group action which significantly enhance their ability to survive in their environments. The mechanisms themselves differ, however. In herd animals, for example, these mechanisms appear to be "hardwired." They are chiefly instinctive, since the interaction patterns do not change with time or place. Human social interactions, on the other hand, are extremely varied in their manifestations, indicating the use of reasoning powers to modify or overcome instinctive patterns.

As noted, human beings have evolved to become members of societies in order to significantly enhance their power over their varied environments. However, human beings require a set of rules of interaction in order to live together successfully in a society. A complete set of such rules of behavior is known as a "culture." Without such rules, individuals would behave according to immediate self-interest and instinct only, and the result would be utter chaos.

Note that adherence to this set of rules does not constitute a "social contract." There is no "agreement" on the part of the individual. The culture is implanted chiefly subconsciously, usually without the individual's "permission." Once the culture has been internalized, the recipient abides by its rules without any further thought. The culture becomes just "the way things are done." It becomes the individual's conscience.

The human social landscape is very complex. It includes a huge number of societies, sub societies, cultures, and subcultures. These groups often entwine, overlap, interact with one another, and have areas of conflict as well. However, the overall characteristics of societies can be explained and understood.

The process of enculturation appears to begin at the mother's breast. A newborn human baby learns very quickly that cooing and suckling are much more successful behaviors and produce much more positive results than biting and roughness. He or she instantly learns how to control this source of nourishment. The process continues in many, many different ways during the stage of infancy – during which the baby is totally dependent upon his or her caregivers. It continues into the relative dependence of early childhood.

These various cultural messages become unconsciously internalized in most individuals. Eventually, they come together as a complete cultural code that defines one's social interactions via accepted cultural norms. However, the basic reason that human beings become enculturated remains our need to control our social and physical environments via the power of membership in a society.

Cultural rules are not all hard and fast. Nor are they all necessary to guarantee a viable society. In fact, some of these rules go far beyond such necessity. Given a broad set of rules for a specific culture, some of them may merely be generally accepted and softly enforced, whereas others may be deemed essential and controlled with physical force. There are all levels of enforcement between these two extremes. And the acceptance and enforcement of cultural rules, along with the rules themselves, vary with time, place, and the specific population.

What we label as "political correctness" are merely proposed alterations to the existing culture which - at least initially - are promoted by a minority of the society's members. Some of these alterations succeed in becoming common parts of the culture; others do not.

The institution that enforces cultural rules with "legitimate" force is generally what we refer to as the government. Although Western cultures typically believe that any force used outside of government sanction is illegitimate, it often occurs nonetheless. In less advanced societies, the distinction between government and civil society is often blurred. In these societies, physical force that is not imposed by the government is often deemed legitimate.

Regardless of the type of society or culture in which individuals find themselves, social bonding by members of a population is essentially a universal trait. The number of humans who exist outside of a social context is negligible.

Culture Modifies Instinctive Drives

As shown in the flow chart, the basic drive to reproduce is modified by culture. Without culturally-applied limits, the drive to reproduce would be a very rough-and-tumble affair, often involving force and injury. Specific cultural limits have a tremendous effect on how this drive is manifested.

The same is true for other instinctive aspects of humans. Culture implants a series of rules of behavior and emotions that combine with "body urges." With the help of knowledge and rationality, the combination results in significant behavior modification. Because of the empathy that culture implants, along with the knowledge that the use of force is illegal, the end result typically does not include force.

If somebody hits you, your instinctive reaction is to hit that person back. However, you may choose not to do so both because you have empathy for the instigator and because you don't want to get into trouble with the law. Of course, a number of other emotional considerations could come into play as well.

A "spectrum" of current and future emotions that come from your culture and your instinctive urges are moderated by the use of knowledge and rationality. Together, they determine your actual reaction to being hit.

Many reproductive acts are criminalized and enforced by the government. For instance, in American society, forceful rape, statutory rape (age restrictions), sexual battery, peeping tomism, indecent exposure, polyandry, polygamy, and even sexual harassment fall into this category. There are many other "soft rules" in the United States that are not illegal but are commonplace. Items that are frowned upon include extramarital sexual relations, extreme age differences, and the viewing of pornography. Other "rules" include some dating conventions and the need to prevent disease in sexual relations.

However, an entire set of different but acceptable reproductive behaviors are part of various other cultures. These cultural rules vary considerably from society to society In fact, they are an area of significant academic study. However, despite their variety, culturally-imposed rules that modify instinctive human urges exist in all societies.

Beliefs - Ethics and Morality

For most people, the idea that cultural values and ethics are implanted through a process that is driven by the need for an individual to control his or her environment is counterintuitive. The process takes place primarily on a sub-conscious level and usually occurs during early childhood. By the time an individual reaches the age of intellectual enlightenment, that person's culture appears to be self-evident and integral to his or her psyche --- almost as if that individual were born with these implants. Once they are embedded in a person, these cultural values and ethics appear to have nothing to do with environmental control. They are merely one's conscience which can always be relied upon.

However, the existence of sociopaths illustrates beyond a doubt that culture/values/ethics of a society are not always implanted successfully. This lack of success is evidence that the process takes place after birth. Although an individual could be born with an inherent tendency to become sociopathic, there are no sociopathic one month olds. Further proof that the process takes place after birth is the fact that there are also no ethical one month olds.

Additional evidence that ethics/morality/values are culturally implanted rather than innate is the fact that they vary greatly from society to society. For example, some societies view the public stoning to death of an adulteress as the work of God. In others, stoning anyone to death at any time for any reason is considered to be cruel and unusual; in fact, it is illegal.

Ethics and morality are a part of culture --- rules of behavior designed to govern interactions between members of a society. Therefore, human ethics is simply a sub-category of human culture. Every human culture has a set of ethical/moral standards that govern interactions between members of that culture. As illustrated above, these sets of ethical standards are by no means uniform; however, all known cultures have some common threads because a set of basic rules is essential for all societies to be viable.

For example, all societies must define the circumstances under which killing one of its members would be considered acceptable behavior. In some societies, this action would never be acceptable. In others, it would be appropriate as an action taken by the government. In still others, the action could be taken by an offended individual, or by a defined social group.

Similarly, all societies need to have some definition of personal property and the rights of property holders. Once again, a great deal of variation exists in this area. In some advanced societies dominated by major property holders, there are well-defined property rights. In less evolved societies, in which ownership is recognized only in cases of current use of the property, the rights either do not exist or are poorly defined. For example, the San people of the Kalahari recognize property rights only for items that are being actively used. If an item is not currently in use, then the principle of "first come, first served" applies.

All societies require definition of a family structure which ensures the enculturation of its children. The structure varies a great deal from society to society, however, ranging from patriarchy to matriarchy to some combination of the two to arrangements in which uncles or aunts have chief responsibility for raising the children. Techniques of family formation also vary widely. In some societies, arranged unions are established at puberty. In others, these unions are self-generated and take place well into adulthood. Some family units are permanent, while others are temporary; some involve multiple partners both serially or in parallel, while others are exclusive.

Cultures are living entities. They change, develop, are destroyed, are created, and die. In addition, some cultures compete with one another. The processes through which cultures progress are very complex; they can only be understood in general terms.

Cultures evolve just as species evolve. A superior culture is one which survives, spreads, and overshadows other cultures. The "best" set of ethics, therefore, is the one that is the most successful.

The social bonding that occurs during enculturation is basically a subconscious mechanism. However, its chief evolutionary value is clear. In return for internalizing and following the rules of a culture, the power of an individual to control his or her physical environment is magnified many times over. Such social bonding also enhances the power of the individual over his or her social environment. If all members of a society adhere to the specified rules of the culture, then the behavior of those members becomes quite predictable. Predictable behavior is much easier to control.

Individual human bonding – in the form of friendship, love, and family -- is an extension of social and cultural bonding. It is essentially the same mechanism; however, it involves either a one-on-one or a few-on-few relationship. In addition, the bonding is significantly intensified. In individual bonding, expectations and predictions of the behavior of others go well beyond the norm of social/cultural predictability. In addition, they usually play a large part in creating the emotions of altruism and empathy.

It might be difficult to see the human qualities of empathy, morality, altruism, and love as being driven by the need for power acquisition. However, they are all derived from the fact that human beings are social animals. The human species radically increases its power over environments by acting in cooperative groups rather than as individuals. As the society increases its power, so too do individuals increase their own power.

Empathy, altruism, love, morality, and ethics are simply the mechanisms required to create a viable human society. They are all activated by the socialization process of early childhood. Because this process normally takes place in a subconscious manner, the individuals involved simply participate in day-to-day life and are unaware that they are working toward the acquisition of power.

In summary, human beings are highly social animals. They can multiply or dramatically extend their individual capabilities and thereby gain control over their environments by bonding in social groups.

Beliefs - Religion

Behold the power of prayer: behave properly and you will be rewarded with everlasting life (or with desirable reincarnation).

Make sacrifices to the gods; dance to make the rain come. If you are ill, make a pilgrimage for a cure. If you fear that which you cannot control, God will help you. Most individuals turn to religious belief of some form because they believe it will allow them to establish control over all that they cannot otherwise control.

Our individual powers give us insufficient control over our environments. We form societies to magnify our powers by building historical knowledge and by group action. However, we are still not completely satisfied because we cannot control ALL aspects of our environments.

But all-knowing and all-powerful god(s) can control the universe as we know it. We know how to influence other members of our societies, so we believe that the techniques for influencing God(s) must be similar. For this reason, we dance, sacrifice, perform rituals, behave properly, and plead (pray).

The prominence of religion in human societies says more about the nature of human beings and their desire to control their environments than it does about the nature of the universe. The need for religion and the ways in which it presents itself vary widely with place and time — from culture to culture. However, religion always serves to fill the gap between the controllable environment (using all of an individual's available powers) and the total human environment.

Ethics/morality is a part of culture that is often tied to, justified by, and/or fortified by religion, but that is not always the case. Many of the more "primitive" religions do not tie ethics or morality to religion. This association occurs most often when the religion of a specific culture or society is threatened by the exposure of its adherents to alternative cultures. It becomes linked to ethics/morality seemingly as a cultural defense mechanism against this competition.

A belief is any presumed knowledge that is not demonstrable by the preponderance of evidence. There are many belief systems that are defined by a culture but are not recognized as religions. Many of these satisfy human needs identical to religion. Some examples include: pet rocks, magic wrist bands, ghosts, gremlins, and rabbit's feet. These can be characterized as simple "superstition," but others are more menacing.

For example, in the early 20th century, the widespread belief that the human propensity to consume alcoholic beverages led to many social evils and could be controlled by government action led to enormous loss of life and large economic losses. This happened because government prohibition of alcohol consumption led to the creation of vast and powerful criminal enterprises.

In the mid-20th century, the beliefs of Stalin, Hitler, and their proponents that their ideologies would lead to major benefits to mankind led to the deaths of millions. These actions proved that human beings are quite willing to commit heinous acts in defense of their belief systems, religious or otherwise.

Many such belief systems exist and their effects range from simple superstition to catastrophic results.

The difference between a belief and knowledge is always a critical question and will likely remain so. No knowledge is totally definitive (factual). Even science is a fluid pursuit. And many beliefs have an apparently factual basis. The answers to the question are incredibly complex: they depend on probabilities, a myriad of contexts, and practicalities. As a result, epistemology remains a vibrant segment of Philosophy. Differing points of view are often more dependent on different perceptions of fact and belief than they are on faulty logic.

All of these beliefs/religions are created to fill the gap between those aspects of the human environment that individuals have the power to control and the entirety of that environment. Historically, as more and more knowledge-based power has accumulated, the cultural importance of religion has decreased. In other words, this accumulation of knowledge has allowed humans to narrow the gap.

However, the gap has not disappeared entirely. Even those individuals who accept as firm knowledge that the world as we know it began with a big bang from something the size of a walnut, the questions of how and why the walnut got there remain. The only alternative that human beings have to exert some control over the gap is to accept/adopt a belief system which addresses it. Religion (or its equivalents) is destined to remain with us for the foreseeable future.

The following chart, entitled "Individual's Total Environment," illustrates the relationship between those aspects of an individual's environment that he or she can control and the gap that is filled by beliefs.

Chart of Individual's Power

Individual's Total Environment

(size of segments is totally arbitrary)

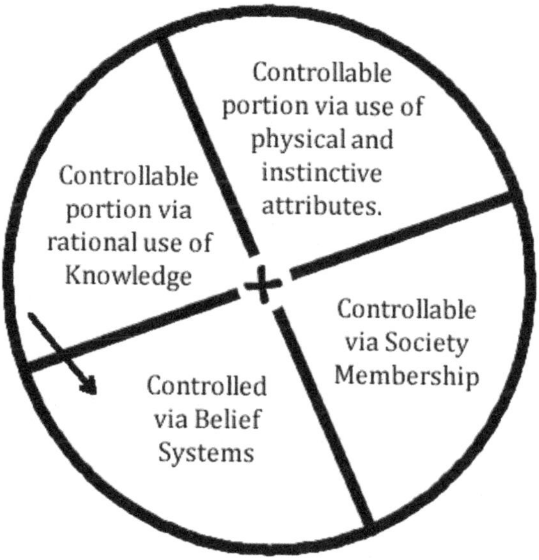

- The individual is driven to control his/her entire environment in order to maximize chances of species survival.
- Portion controlled by knowledge is vastly enhanced by society membership. Society membership requires enculturation.
- Knowledge portion is constantly growing via social transmission and creation of new knowledge.
- Portion controlled by physical and instinctive capabilities is relatively constant (slow or no evolution).
- Portion controlled by Belief Systems constantly shrinks as knowledge portion increases.
- Belief Systems fill the gap between the total environment and the portions that can be controlled via the physical or rational.

A person buying ordinary products in a supermarket is in touch with his deepest emotions.

--John Kenneth Galbraith

Emotions to Actions

The Creation of Emotions

Emotions are derived from four major sources: (1) the physical and instinctive attributes of the individual; (2) the culture implanted in the individual (chiefly in the subconscious) by his or her society; (3) the beliefs implanted in the individual, and (4) the individual's inherent drive to reproduce (modified by culture).

Physical and instinctive attributes generally give rise to both what we colloquially call "feelings" and some of what we colloquially call "emotions." (For the purpose of this essay, we have defined "emotions" as including both feelings and emotions.) Feelings of hunger, thirst, heat, cold, and biological necessities of all types are the obvious result of our physical nature. Instinctively, we avoid some things and are attracted to others. For example, we would generally avoid an environment that posed physical danger, such as fire, high places, enclosed spaces, or snakes. On the other hand, we would likely seek out environments that contained pleasant temperatures and comfortable, safe places, or ones with soft, furry non-aggressive animals.

Our drive to reproduce is an obvious source of a whole range of emotions, many of which have been well documented and are very powerful motivators. A detailed rehash is unnecessary. The emotions that are the result of the drive to reproduce are often significantly modified or influenced by the culture transmitted by the society to which an individual belongs. For example, cultural modification of the base drive often turns the instinct to forcibly engage in sexual relations into the instinct to seduce another individual via persuasion. Similarly, cultural influences can change the instinct to reproduce almost indiscriminately into a desire to engage in the activity of reproduction only under very specific circumstances.

Emotions that are derived through cultural influences, however, are often less easy to see. Because much of culture is implanted in our subconscious mind during early childhood, these types of emotions often appear to be fundamental to our makeup or inherited. Different cultures create different sets of emotions with differing strengths. In one extreme case, for example, a woman who commits adultery in tribal Pakistan triggers such strong emotions that she may end up being stoned -- possibly to death. In the United States, on the other hand, such behavior may be frowned upon by some, but any severe public emotions are rarely expressed. There are many other examples, of course. Dismembering the hands of convicted thieves in Saudi Arabia is another example. Most examples of this phenomenon are much less severe, however.

Emotions Motivate All Actions

Emotions are the motivating factors in all choices and decisions that human beings make. These choices and decisions, in turn, lead to all human actions. You can test this statement by repeatedly asking yourself "why" you or anyone has made a specific decision or taken a specific action until you get to the most basic reasons.

For example, a person who purchases a new car is likely to narrow the choice down to choosing between car A and car B. The individual chooses car A. Why? He may make that choice because car A has a more powerful engine and costs slightly less than car B. The individual appears to have made a rational decision.

Let's back up this decision a step and ask why the individual values a more powerful engine. He may state that a more powerful engine will allow him to accelerate more quickly at traffic lights and when passing another car. Once again, the decision appears to be rational. Let's keep going and ask why he wants to accelerate more quickly at traffic lights and when passing another car. The answer may be that the faster acceleration will allow him to get around slower vehicles and to arrive at his destination earlier. Again, the explanation appears to be rational.

Why does he want to arrive earlier? Perhaps he needs to arrive at an appointment on time or would like extra time to do something else before a scheduled appointment. Why does he want to be on time for appointments? Because he may insult the person with whom he has the appointment, or he may receive a poor performance evaluation at his job if he is very late. The reason why he doesn't want to insult another person is that it will make him feel guilty. We have reached one of the basic drivers of the decision to buy car A and it is an emotion!

The other core reason that this individual gave is a desire for a positive job evaluation - basically a monetary cause. Note that the other reason that the individual gave originally for choosing car A was also monetary. If you conduct a similar "why" analysis of monetary causes, you will also end in the expression of emotions(s). If you are unsure that this statement is correct, try asking "why" at each stage of a decision-making process until you reach the base emotion.

What do we mean when we say colloquially that someone has made an "emotional decision"? What do we mean when we say that someone has made a "rational decision"?

Since all decisions are emotionally driven in the final analysis, truly rational decisions do not exist. Judging a decision to be rational is based on superficial appearances, rather than on any attempt to understand basic motivations.

When base emotions are deeply embedded and are revealed only by the type of extensive analysis we did in our car example, we colloquially refer to that as a "rational decision." When the emotional drivers are easily discernible, we refer to that as an "emotional decision." Immediately discernible emotions tend to be those that currently exist. Future probable emotions tend to be buried more deeply. And deeply embedded emotions tend to be those that we can predict for the future, such as the example of being late for an appointment in the analysis above.

Only human beings have the ability to rationally balance and maximize the satisfaction of a spectrum of current and future emotions. This rational analysis includes both the perceived strength of each emotion that makes up the spectrum and the probability that specific future emotions will actually occur.

The complex rational analysis of predicting the strengths and probabilities of a complex set of emotions and balancing them against a current spectrum of emotions is typically done almost instantaneously; it also occurs primarily on a subconscious level. As noted above, a dog will always go for the steak that is currently on the table, regardless of probable future negative emotional consequences, because he is unable to predict those future emotions and the probability of their occurring. A human being, on the other hand, will do the analysis before taking action.

Debate and divergence of views can only enrich our history and culture.

--Ibrahim Babangida

Conclusions

- The human species requires reproduction in order to survive. No individuals live forever. As a result, individuals must survive long enough to reproduce and nurture their offspring to independence.

- The primary survival technique for a human individual is to exercise control over that individual's environment (broadly defined).

- The power to control an individual's environment is largely limited to the human species. Other species primarily use other survival techniques, such as rapid maturation, multiple reproduction, and rapid evolution.

- There are two basic human drives: (1) the drive to reproduce and (2) the drive to have the power to control one's environment. They are designed to assure survival of the species via procreation.

- There are three sources of human power: (1) physical and instinctive attributes, (2) knowledge and rational thinking ability, and (3) membership in a human society. The latter source multiplies individual power via cooperative effort and the transmission of accumulated knowledge.

- Membership in a society vastly enhances individual power. However, it also requires that the individual acquire the CULTURE of the society. Thus, membership in a society is contingent upon acquisition of its culture.

- Acquisition of culture is largely internalized in the subconscious mind; it occurs primarily during early childhood. Cultural acquisition includes a broad spectrum of rules of behavior and beliefs, most of which remain unquestioned in an individual's lifetime. Failure of an individual to acquire the cultural norms through this process can lead to sociopathy. The basic drives lead to emotional motivations in a complex manner. The causal chain is not self-evident because much of the connection between the two involves social enculturation, primarily via the subconscious mind.

- Social enculturation has two functions for the individual. First, it prevents the individual's use of his or her raw power exclusively for self-interest. Second, it vastly increases the power available to the society's individuals.

- Many human attributes which are widely admired and seem to have no relationship to the drive for power are acquired during the enculturation process. These include cooperation, love, friendship, compassion, sympathy, altruism, and many others. The tendency to acquire these attributes may be inherited, but they are not in-born qualities; enculturation is required. For that reason, there are no altruistic one month olds.

- All human action decisions are based on human emotions (broadly defined). Take any real or hypothetical human action and ask what motivated it. The first answer to the question is likely to sound logical. If you keep asking what motivated a specific decision or action, eventually the train of questions will stop at an emotion or a set of emotions.

- The ability to think rationally is a tool that is used to understand, analyze, and prioritize spectrums of both current and probable future emotions which may be satisfied by a decision or an act. The colloquial description of a "rational decision" refers to an attempt to create a balance of current and probable future emotions that is most useful for survival. On the other hand, an "emotional decision" refers to a decision based on current emotions only. Note that there are no purely rational decisions.

- Emotions have four sources: (1) an individual's inherent physical and instinctive attributes (usually called "feelings"), (2) the drive to reproduce (which has been analyzed extensively), (3) the drive to enhance power over the individual's environment, and (4) the individual's acquired culture. All four of these sources of emotions are keyed to the survival of an individual.

- Human beings are inherently motivated to exercise power/control over all aspects of their environment. However, human powers are insufficient to cover all aspects of their physical and social environments. There is a gap between the total environment and what can be controlled via knowledge and society membership. This gap is normally filled with belief systems – often in the form of religions – which become part of the enculturation process.

Selected References

Boole, George. "The Laws of Thought," Cambridge University Press, 1854, 2009.

Bowlby, John. "Attachment," New York: Basic Books, 1969, 1999.

Freud, Sigmund. "A General Introduction to Psychoanalysis," 1924. Barnes and Noble, New York

Herskovitz, M.J. "Cultural Anthropology," New York: Random House, 1955.

Hofstede, Geert J. "Cultures and Organizations," New York: McGraw Hill, 2005.

Hofstede, Geert J. "Culture's Consequences," Beverly Hills, CA: Sage Publications, 1980.

Smith, John Maynard. "The Theory of Evolution," London: Penguin Books, 1958.

Sowell, Thomas. "Conquest and Cultures: an International History," New York: Basic Books, 1998.

Wood, James W. "The Dynamics of Human Reproduction," New Brunswick, New Jersey: Aldine Transaction Publishers, 1994.

Wunsch, A. David. "First Hand: An Electrical Engineering Education at Cornell 1956 to 1961," Engineering Technology and History Wiki <ethw.org>, 2015.

About The Author

In his ¾ of a century, Robert Boysen has had the advantages of a self-reliant upbringing, a very broad education, extensive people management experience, and exposure to a wide variety of human cultures. All of these factors together have led to the current work.

Bob was born in Princeton, New Jersey, in 1940 and raised in rustic countryside about 6 miles from Princeton. Electricity and telephone services reached his home when he was 9 years old.

He chose the five-year Mechanical Engineering program at Rutgers University, earning a Bachelor of Science degree and a Bachelor of Arts degree. He completed his broad education with a Master of Science degree in Management at the New Jersey Institute of Technology.

Bob had a 35-year career as a research scientist, research manager, and business manager in a Fortune 100 company. His business travels in the field of technology licensing and sales took him to 24 countries. During his career, he was awarded eight patents and published ten technical articles.

Bob's physically-oriented hobby pursuits included sailing, bicycling, white water canoeing, flying, and hiking. People management experience and broad culture exposure continued to be enhanced via his development of small group bicycle tours and charter sail cruises. The former included 55 group bicycle tours in 28 countries totaling 28,000 miles. The latter included skippering 27 charters for a total of 180 days in 13 countries;

Bob has spent much of his time since his retirement in volunteer people-management positions with three non-profit organizations in the fields of bicycling, hiking, and business management. He has also created and published several bicycling maps, and a trail guidebook of the Kittatinny Mountains, as well as designing and building three private homes.

A lifelong resident of New Jersey, Bob has been married to Rose Marie for 52 years; they have one daughter. Bob and his wife currently live on a forty-acre farm in rural northwest New Jersey.

Acknowledgements

Karen Misler for excellent and extensive developmental editing.

Bruce Thomson and. Lenny Scarola for partial critiques of earlier even more baffling versions.

Publisher -- folks at First Edition Design Publishing